C is for Carbon

Written by: Marilee Summers M.Ed

Illustrated by: Kimberlee Wojtko

Published by MackStorm Productions
348 Donna Lane
Bloomingdale, IL 60108

Illustrated by Kimberlee Wojtko

Text set in Comic Sans
Printed in the USA on acid-free paper

Publisher's Cataloging-in-Publication
(Provided by Quality books, Inc.)

Summers, Marilee.
    C is for carbon / written by Marilee Summers;
illustrated by Kimberlee Wojtko.
    p. cm.
    Includes bibliographical references.
    SUMMARY: Simplifies the field of chemistry and
introduces 26 of the 118 known carbon elements.
    Audience: Ages 2-14.

    ISBN 0-9753078-0-0

    1. Carbon--Juvenile literature. [1. Carbon.]
I. Wojtko, Kimberlee. II. Title.

QD181.C1S86 2005   546'.681
                                    QBI05-800224

        ISBN: 0-9753078-0-0

Thank you,

...without their inspiration, love & support this would not be possible.

A special thank you to Peter Cokic PhD. and Farrel Summers PhD. for your editing and suggestions.

MACKStorm
Productions, Inc.
www.MackStormProductions.com

The primary goal of this picture book is to introduce early readers, teachers, moms and dads to the chemical elements. They are here, what you are sitting on and all around us. There are nearly 118 known elements. They are the building blocks that create life. When they touch together they are the air we breathe, dirt, cars, feet, butter, stars and on & on. They make up all matter, which means you, me and everything!

The second purpose is to get the supplied poster of The Periodic Table up and in front of your child. Each of our chemical friends has a special relationship with it's neighbor on the chart. Position and location are very important. Our friends have personalities, relationships and desires. Just like learning a new language seeing this chart **early and often** helps us prepare for future understanding.

This is a see it and say it book. Parents and teachers can read the names aloud, point out the chemical symbols, count the stars (electrons) and look and see where each element can be found. Encourage children to say the name out-loud and recognize the element's symbol. Phonetic pronunciation break downs are provided on each page. In addition, in the back of this book is a list of Great Resources to promote learning in the field of chemistry.

And on the first day God commanded, "Let there be light and there was light." With His words He set the sun in the heavens and from our sun His building blocks were formed...the elements.

Please enjoy this first in a series of adventures in chemistry.

Al is for . . .

Aluminum

Can you say ... ah-LOO-men-em ?

4

I am in ....

cans

airplanes

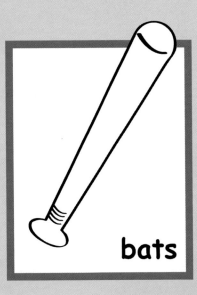

bats

bikes

and more.

5

B is for . . .

Boron

I am in ...

plants

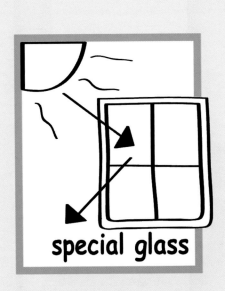

special glass

eye drops

tennis rackets

and more.

7

C is for . . .

Carbon

I am in ...

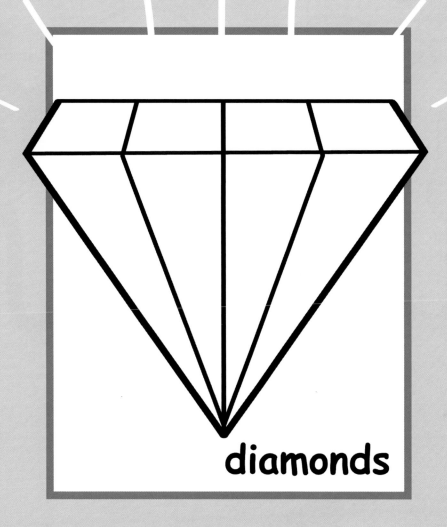

diamonds

pencils

people

plastic things

and more.

Dy is for...

Dysprosium

Can you say ... dis-PRO-zee-em ?

I am in ...

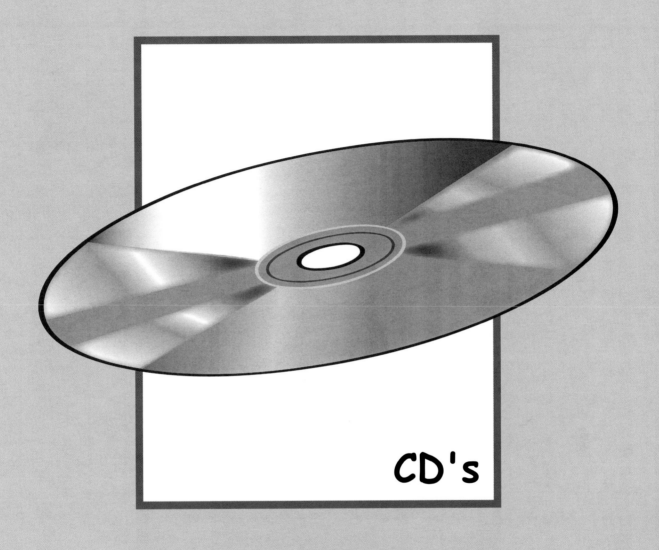

CD's

magnets

color tv's

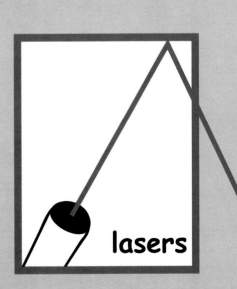

lasers

and more.

Es is for...

99

99

Es

Einsteinium

Can you say ... ine-STINE-ee-em ?

I am in ...

the waste of a
nuclear explosion

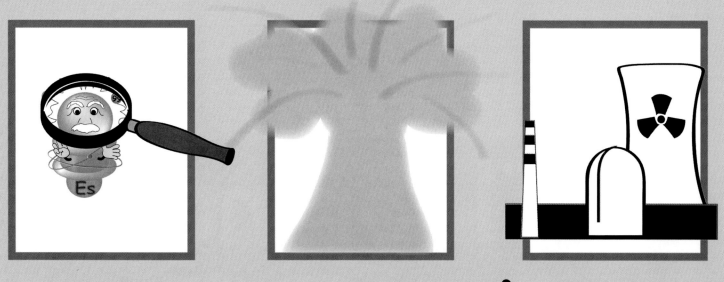

and more.

F is for . . .

Fluorine

Can you say . . . FLOOR-een ?

I am in ...

toothpaste

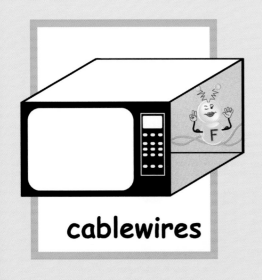

cablewires

bug spray

energy

and more.

Ga is for...

Gallium

Can you say ... GAL-ee-em ?

I am in ...

calculators

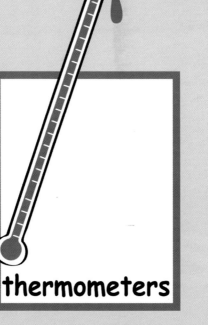

thermometers

mirrors

computers

and more.

H is for . . .

Hydrogen

Can you say . . . HI-dro-jen . . . ?

I am in ...

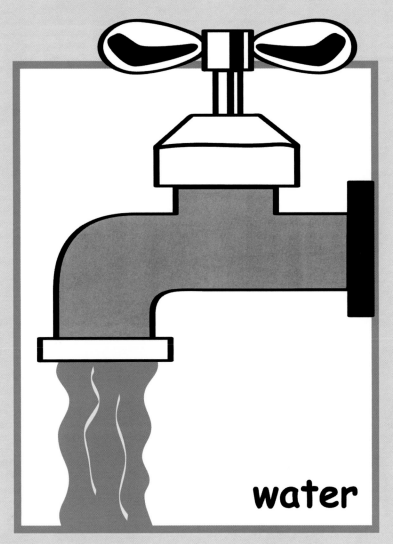

water

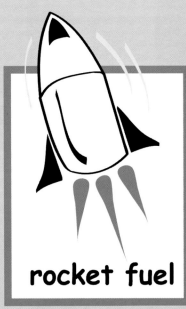

rocket fuel

CHOCOLATE

candy bars

stars

and more.

I is for...

Iodine

Can you say ... EYE-eh-dine ?

I am in ...

our body

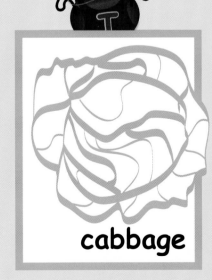

cabbage

dirt

milk

and more.

J is for...

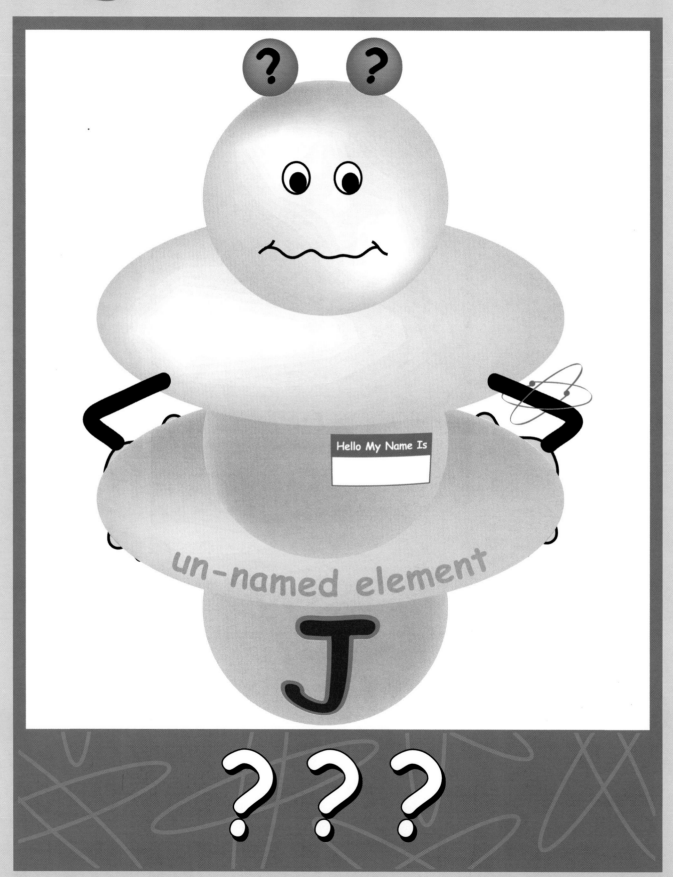

J

un-named element

Hello My Name Is

???

22

Where will we find J?

Add your artwork in these boxes.

Kr is for . . .

Krypton

Can you say ... KRIP-ton ?

I am in ...

Mars' atmosphere

flash bulbs

neon lights

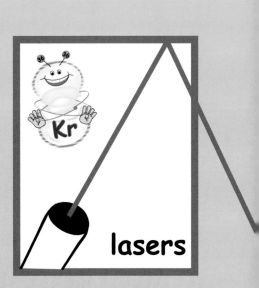

lasers

and more.

Li is for ...

Lithium

Can you say ... LITH-ee-em ?

I am in ...

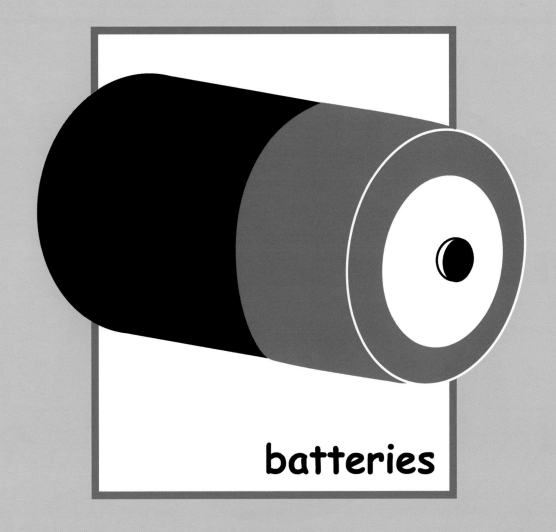

batteries

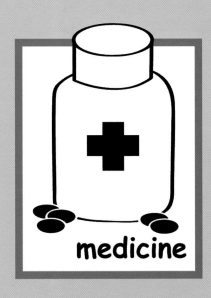

medicine

potatoes

trains

and more.

Mg is for...

Magnesium

Can you say ... mag-NEE-zee-em ?

I am in ...

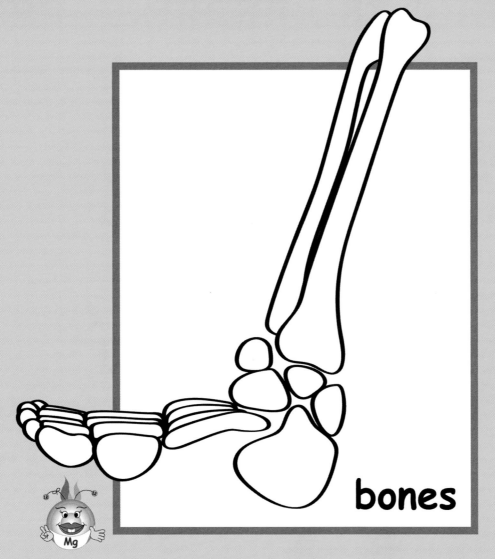

bones

bricks

nuts

fish

and more.

N is for . . .

Nitrogen

Can you say ... NYE-dro-jen ?

I am in ...

smog (pollution)

deer antlers

whipped cream cans

brains

and more.

O is for . . .

Oxygen

Can you say ... AAK-see-jen ?

I am in ...

air

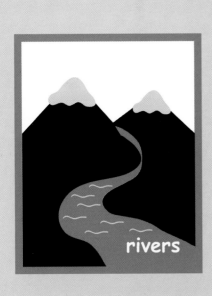

rivers

fire

dogs

and more.

P is for . . .

Phosphorus

Can you say ... FOS-fer-us?

I am in ...

children

cake

soap

eggs

and more.

Uuq is for...

Uuq

Ununquadium

Can you say ... un-un-QUAD-ee-em?

I am in ...

a nuclear reaction

  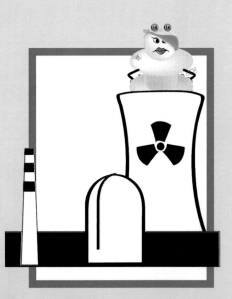

and more.

Rn is for . . .

Radon

Can you say . . . RAY-don ?

I am in ...

rocks

medicine

the earth

basements

and more.

39

S is for...

Sulfur

Can you say ... SUL-fer ?

I am in ...

the skunk's smell

diet pop

all living things

the moon and earth

and more.

Tl is for...

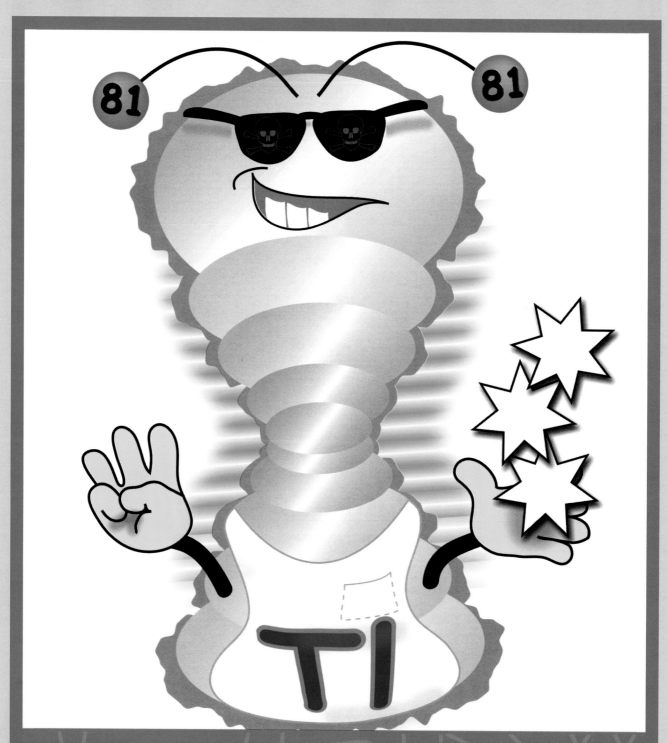

Thallium

Can you say ... THAL-ee-em ?

I am in ...

heart medicine

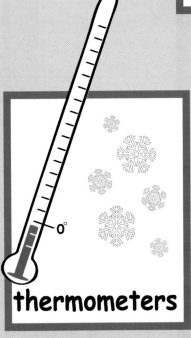

thermometers

water pollution

poison

and more.

U is for ...

Uranium

Can you say ... yoo-RAY-nee-em ?

I am in ...

fuel

the earth

submarines

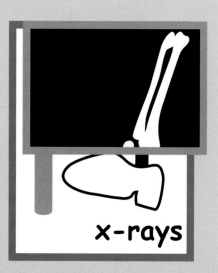

x-rays

and more.

V is for...

Vanadium

Can you say ... veh-NAY-dee-em ?

I am in ...

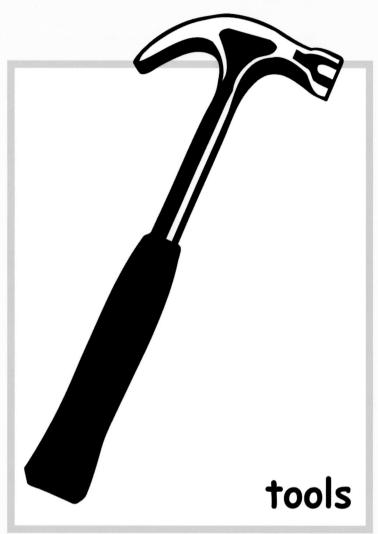

tools

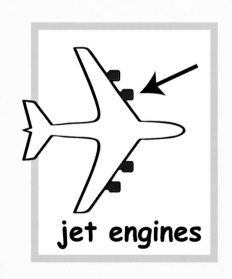

jet engines

sun flowers

seafood

and more.

W is for...

Wolfram*

*Commonly known as Tungsten

Can you say ... WOOL-frem ?

I am in ...

light bulbs

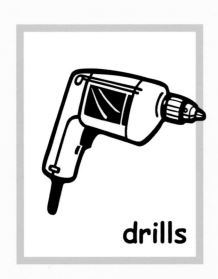

drills

trees

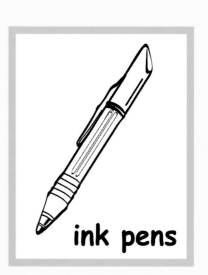

ink pens

and more.

Xe is for...

Xe

Xenon

Can you say ... ZEE-non ?

I am in ...

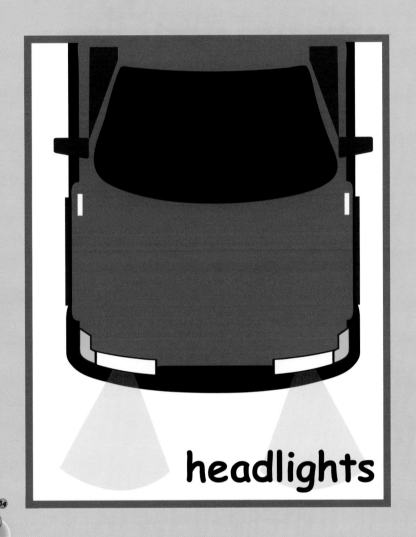

headlights

movie projectors

flash bulbs

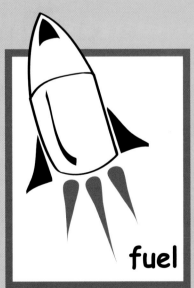

fuel

and more.

Y is for...

Yttrium

Can you say ... IT-ree-em?

I am in ...

a camera lens

the moon

tiles

microwave ovens

and more.

Zn is for . . .

Zinc

Can you say ... ZINk ?

I am in ...

toys

sweet corn

sun block

horns

and more.

Character Specifications

	Shirt Design	Antenna Balls	Stars	Arm Length	Antenna Style	Size	Color	Shape	Features
	Symbol	Atomic No.	Bonding Electrons	EA (Electron Affinity)	EN (Electron Givity)	Atomic Radius	Color at Ambient	Bonding Orbital	Characteristics
Aluminum ■	Al	13	3	0.43	1.61	143	Silvery/Bluish White	$3p^1$	Bendable, malleable, soft, light-weight, friendly and very reactive metal
Boron ■	B	5	3	0.28	2.04	80	Brownish Black Powder	$2p^1$	Jeckyl & Hyde - Mimics metals & Non-metals, shapeless powder - Is never found alone
Carbon ■	C	6	4	1.26	2.55	77	Black & Transparent	$2p^2$	Popular, makes long chains of herself, she has 4 versions and is the basis of life
Dysprosium ■	Dy	66	3	0.50	1.22	175	Silvery/Bright White	$4f^{10}$	Very soft, resists heat and hard to find
Einsteinium ■	Es	99	3	0.50	1.30	203	Silvery/Grayish White	$5f^{11}$	Man-made, radioactive and named after Albert Einstein
Florine 🎈	Es	99	7	3.40	3.98	71	Pale Yellow/Greenish	$2p^5$	Most aggressively seeking electrons, corrosive, intense and has a bad odor
Gallium 〰	Ga	31	3	0.43	1.81	122	Silvery Blue	$4p^1$	Used to make mirrors, at room temperature between a solid/liquid
Hydrogen 🎈	H	1	1	0.75	2.20	37	Colorless	$1s^1$	Very samll, light weight, friendly forming lasting/strong relationships
Iodine ■	I	53	7	3.06	2.66	133	Bluish/Black	$5p^3$	Emits a bluish/violet gas and aggressively seeks other
Krypton 🎈	Kr	36	8	0.00	0.00	103	Colorless	$4p^6$	In the lab shows green and orange spectral lines - Happy and stable
Lithium ■	Li	3	1	0.62	0.98	152	Silvery with Black Crust	$2s^1$	Forms a black crust when exposed to air - wants to make friends
Magnesium ■	Mg	12	2	0.00	1.31	160	Silvery/White Grayish	$3s^2$	Catches on fire and tarnishes when exposed to air - Easily makes friends
Nitrogen 🎈	N	7	5	0.07	3.04	74	Colorless	$2p^3$	Sluggish, stable and likes to be with other Nitrogen's
Oxygen 🎈	O	8	6	1.46	3.44	74	Colorless	$2p^4$	Friendly, likes being with other O's - At very cold temperatures it appears blue
Phosphorus ■	P	15	5	0.75	2.19	110	White to Yellow	$3p^3$	Waxy, very friendly, must be kept under water or he will heat up in air
Ununquadium ■	Uuq	114	4	Unknown	Unknown	Unknown	Silvery/White Graysih	$7p^2$	Lab made, little known, thought to be a member of the danerous P block gang
Radon 🎈	Rn	86	8	0.00	0.00	134	Colorless	$6p^6$	Emits alpha rays, son of Radium, few friends, orange at very cold temps
Sulfer ■	S	16	6	2.08	2.58	103	Pale Yellow	$3p^4$	Little known, mysterious and comes in 4 different forms
Thallium ■	Tl	81	3	0.20	1.80	170	Silvery White w/Gray Tinge	$6p^1$	Ting of blue in air, emits green spectral lines, bad boy P Block Gang Member
Uranium ■	U	92	7	Unknown	1.70	139	Silvery White Grayish	$5f^3$	"The Grandfather" As he decays becomes another, has heat and alpha rays
Vanadium ■	V	23	5	0.53	1.63	131	Bright White/Silvery Gray	$3d^3$	Slightly radioactive, name= Swedish Goddess, gives colors to ceramics
Wolfram* ■	W	74	6	0.82	1.70	137	Steely Gray to Bright White	$5d^4$	Strong - has the highest melting point- gives strength to others
Xenon 🎈	Xe	54	8	0.00	2.60	218	Colorless	$5p^6$	Stable and happy - Name= Stranger (hard to find) when excited glows blue
Yttrium ■	Y	39	3	0.31	1.22	179	Silvery	$4d^1$	If exposed to air forms a protective film- Makes the "Red" color in our TVs
Zinc ■	Zn	30	2	0.09	1.65	133	Pale Gray-Bluish White	$3d^{10}$	Super platicity, bends and twists - Tarnishes when exposed to air

*Wolfram is commonly known as Tungsten

Key: ■=solid 🎈=gas 〰=liquid

56

The Entire Cast of 118 Elements

Name	Pronunciation	Symbol	Name	Pronunciation	Symbol
Actinium	ak-TIN-ee-em	Ac	Neon	NEE-ON	Ne
Aluminum	al-LOO-min-um	Al	Neptunium	nep-TOO-nee-em	Np
Americium	am-er-ISS-ee-em	Am	Nickel	NIK-el	Ni
Antimony	an-ta-MONY	Sb	Niobium	ni-O-bee-em	Nb
Argon	AR-gon	Ar	Nitrogen	NYE-trh-jen	N
Arsenic	AR-sa-nik	As	Nobelium	no-BELL-ee-em	No
Astatine	AS-ta-teen	At	Osmium	OZ-me-em	Os
Barium	BARE-ee-em	Ba	Oxygen	AAK-see-jen	O
Berkelium	berk-EEL-ee-em	Bk	Palladium	pa-LAY-dee-em	Pd
Beryllium	ba-RIL-ee-em	Be	Phosphorus	FOS-fer-us	P
Bismuth	BI-muth	Bi	Platinum	PLAT-n-em	Pt
Bohrium	BORE-ee-em	Bh	Plutonium	ploo-TOE-nee-em	Pu
Boron	BOR-on	B	Polonium	ps-LO-nee-em	Po
Bromine	BRO-meen	Br	Potassium	poh-TASS-ee-em	K
Cadmium	KAD-mee-em	Cd	Praseodymium	PRA-zee-o-DIM-ee-em	Pr
Calcium	KAL-see-em	Ca	Promethium	pro-ME-thee-em	Pm
Californium	KAL-a-FOR-nee-em	Cf	Protactinium	PRO-tac-TIN-ee-em	Pa
Carbon	CAR-ben	C	Radium	RAY-dee-em	Ra
Cerium	SIR-ee-em	Ce	Radon	Ray-don	Rn
Cesium	SEE-zee-em	Cs	Rhenium	REE-nee-em	Re
Chlorine	KLOR-een	Cl	Rhodium	ROW-dee-em	Rh
Chromium	KRO-mee-em	Cr	Roentgenium	RENT-gen-ee-em	Rg
Cobalt	KO-BALT	Co	Rubidium	roo-BID-ee-em	Rb
Copper	KOP-er	Cu	Ruthenium	roo-THEE-nee-em	Ru
Curium	CURIE-ee-em	Cm	Rutherfordium	RUTH-er-FOR-dee-em	Rf
Darmstadtium	DARM-stat-ee-em	Ds	Samarium	sa-MAR-ee-em	Sm
Dubnium	DUB-nee-em	Db	Scandium	SCAN-dee-em	Sc
Dysprsium	dis-PRO-zee-em	Dy	Seaborgium	see-BORG-ee-em	Sg
Einsteinium	ine-STINE-ee-em	Es	Selenium	sa-lee-nee-em	Se
Erbium	ER-bee-em	Er	Silicon	SIL-i-con	Si
Europium	yoo-ROW-pee-em	Eu	Silver	SIL-ver	Ag
Fermium	FUR-me-em	Fm	Sodium	SO-dee-em	Na
Fluorine	FLOOR-een	F	Strontium	STRON-chee-em	Sr
Francium	FRAN-see-em	Fr	Sulfer	SUL-fer	S
Gadolinium	GAD-oh-lin-ee-em	Gd	Tantalum	TAN-ta-lum	Ta
Gallium	GAL-ee-em	Ga	Technetium	tek-NEE-see-em	Tc
Germanium	jer-MAY-nee-em	Ge	Tellurium	ta-LOOR-ee-em	Te
Gold	GOLD	Au	Terbium	TER-bee-em	Tb
Hafnium	HAF-nee-em	Hf	Thallium	THAL-ee-em	Tl
Hassium	HASS-ee-em	Hs	Thorium	THOR-ee-em	Th
Helium	HE-lee-em	He	Thulium	THOO-lee-em	Tm
Holmium	HOL-mee-em	Ho	Tin	TIN	Sn
Hydrogen	HI-dro-jen	H	Titanium	tie-TAY-nee-em	Ti
Indium	i-RID-ee-em	Ir	Uranium	yoo-RAY-nee-em	U
Iron	I-ern	Fe	Ununbium	un-un-BEE-em	Uub
Krypton	KRIP-ton	Kr	Ununhexium	un-un-HEX-ee-em	Uuh
Lanthanum	LAN-than-em	La	Ununoctium	un-un-OCT-tee-em	Uuo
Lawrencium	law-REN-see-em	Lr	Ununpentium	un-un-PEN-TEE-em	Uut
Lead	LED	Pb	Ununquadium	un-un-QUAD-ee-em	Uuq
Lithium	LITH-ee-em	Li	Ununseptium	un-un-SEP-TEE-em	Uus
Lutetium	loo-TE-she-em	Lu	Ununtrium	un-un-TRY-em	Uut
Magnesium	mag-NEE-zee-em	Mg	Vanadium	veh-NAY-dee-em	V
Manganese	MANG-ga-neez	Mn	Wolfram*	WOOL-frem	W
Meitnerium	MIT-neer-ee-em	Mt	Xenon	ZEE-non	Xe
Mendelevium	men-da-LEE-vee-em	Md	Ytterbium	i-TUR-bee-em	Yb
Mercury	MURK-yoo-ree	Hg	Yttrium	IT-ree-em	Y
Molybdenum	mol-IB-den-em	Mo	Zinc	ZINK	Zn
Neodymium	NEE-o-DIM-ee-em	Nd	Zirconium	zur-COE-nee-em	Zr

WHITE STARS
= Electrons

White Stars – *(Introducing Valence Electrons)*

The stars around each element are very important. They represent electrons or specifically the total valence (vay-lens) electrons. Valence electrons are those electrons that are available for bonding with others and they have the highest energy level. These stars or valence electrons are ready to jump, react, bond to make a friendship at a moments notice. True happiness for an element is to have "8" electrons called an octet (aK-tet). They will grab, share or give up electrons to have their magic "8." The Periodic Table helps us see the special number of valence electrons for each element.

Go to The Periodic Table and find the Roman Numerals above each column. By looking at the Roman Numerals you can see how many valence electrons are in each element in the column below. Elements in the same column have the same number of Valence electrons and behave or "act" in the same way.

COLOR =
At Room Tempreture

Color – *(Introducing Ambient)*

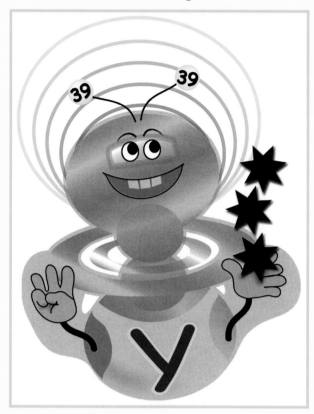

We did our best to give the elements their true color. Whenever possible we used the color of each element at room temperature. When something is at room temperature we say it is at ambient (am-BEE-ant) temperature. Most of the elements on The Periodic Table are metallic or silver at ambient temperature. To help distinguish one from another we made enhancements based on other chemical characteristics and uses. We found elements that were in their gaseous form to be challenging.

BLACK STARS = Electrons

Black Stars - Are also valence electrons. Some elements do not follow the rules or law of The Periodic Table so we gave them black stars or electrons. The Transition elements and those in the Lanthanide and Actinide Groups are very large in size. When it comes to electrons it is this big size that makes them unique and allows them special flexibility.

SIZE = Atomic Radius

Size - *(Introducing The Atomic Radius) AR*

The sizing of our 26 friends is based on Atomic Radius. AR is the measure of half the distance between the nuclei of two atoms of a pure element. This distance is very small and is measured in units called nanometers (NM). Special X-ray equipment is used to make the measurement.

The Periodic Table helps us see this size relationship. Elements at the top of the chart have a smaller AR then those at the bottom. Elements on the left side of the chart are larger then those on the right side. This is called the "Snowman Rule." The element's AR is like the round balls of the snowman that get bigger toward the bottom. Now imagine the snowman falling to the right. Bigger left and smaller right! Of our 26 friends Hydrogen has the smallest AR and Xenon has the largest.

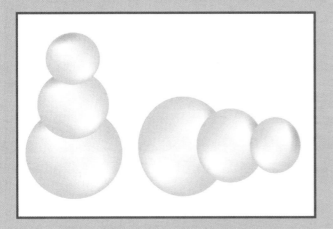

ARM LENGTH = Strength

Arm length - *(Introducing Electron Affinity)*

Notice that the arm length on each element is not the same. This is because it represents that element's electron affinity (a-FIN-a-tee). Electron affinity tells us the amount of attraction to other element's electrons. Remember that all of our friends want to have the magic number "8" electrons to complete their octet. The elements with the longest arms are the strongest grabbers. They really want electrons or stars. No arms or very short arms are the weakest grabbers. Some of the weaker grabbers (short arms) are not interested in other electrons. They will need help or energy to make a grab.

SHAPE = Where Electrons are found
Shape - *(Introducing The Atomic Orbital)*

The images of each of our characters is based on each elements particular atomic orbital structure. An atomic orbital is the space, most likely where we would find electrons at a given energy level. What happens is electrons move around and create a specific cloud-like shape. We used these cloud-like shapes as bodies for each of our elemental friends. Orbital shapes can change when more energy is applied and the electrons move rapidly distorting the cloud or when bonding occurs. However, for our characters we chose a restful and simplified orbital structure.

ANTENNAS
= How They Share

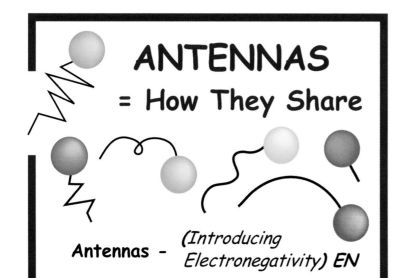

Antennas – *(Introducing Electronegativity)* **EN**

Look at the antennas for each of our elemental friends. You will see six different types. Each of these represents the element's electronegativity. This (ee-LEK-tro-NEG-a-tiv-a-TEE) is all about sharing. Remember that the elements are trying to get the magic number "8" stars or electrons. To do this they must share electrons. When they share the elements hold hands and form a bond but the elements are not fair sharers!

Some are stronger and pull the electrons closer to themselves. They are still stuck together but one may be hogging the electrons! This pulling strength is given a number from 0 to 4. Fluorine pulls the hardest and has an electronegativity of 4. The antenna styles help you see who hogs and pulls electrons the most. See the key below.

ANTENNA BALLS =
Atomic Number

Antenna Balls – *(Introducing The Atomic Number)*

The number inside the ball at the end of each antenna is the atomic number. Each element has its own atomic number. To get this number we count the number of protons in the nucleus. The nucleus is located in the center of the element. Think of the nucleus like the element's heart that has protons in it. Electrons move or orbit around the nucleus (heart). When you have a nucleus containing protons with orbiting electrons you call it an atom. The Periodic Table is arranged by atomic number (or proton count), from the smallest to the largest.

NAMING
J – *(The Un-named Element)*

Currently there is no element beginning with the letter "J" or "Q." However, element's 112-118 are waiting to be named and have temporary names. New names will be given by **The International Union of Pure and Applied Chemistry** (IUPAC). The names are generally famous scientists who discovered the element or towns where the element was discovered. Naming these new elements is not easy. Many people have strong feelings about elements 112-118. You could be the future scientist to discover a new element like 119 & 120!

ANTENNA KEY (strength of pulling when sharing) EN

ANTENNA STYLE		PULLING & HOGGING STRENGTH
Straight	=	None
Wilted	=	Tiny
Curvy	=	Small
Loopy	=	Medium
Zig Zag	=	Great
Extreme Zig Zag	=	Greatest

Books

Dickson,   T.R. Introduction to Chemistry, 8th edition. John Wiley & Sons., 1999

Emsley,   John. Nature's Building Blocks. New York, NY: Oxford University Press Inc., 2002

Emsley,   John. The Elements. New York, NY: Osfod University Press Inc., 2000

Holtzclaw,   Henry F. Jr., Robinson, William R and Nebergall, William H. College Chemistry with Qualitive Anaysis, 7th edition. Lexington, MA & Toronto Canada: D.C. health and Company, 1984

Hunt,   Andrew. Dictionary of Chemistry. Chicago, IL: Fitzroy Dearborn Publishers, 1999

Knapp,   Brian. Elements, vols 1-18. Danbury, CT: Grolier Educational, Sherman Turnpike, 1996

Krebs,   Robert E. The history and Use of Our Earth's Chemical Elements: A Reference Guide. Greenwood Press, 1998

Lide,   David R. CRC Handbook of Chemistr and Physics, 84th edition. Boca Raton, FL: CRC Press, 2003

Newton,   David E. Chemical Elements, vols 1-3. Farmington Hills, MI: Gale Group, 2000

Mader,   Sylvia S. Biology, 8th edition. New York, NY: McGraw-Hill, 2004

Stwertka,   Albert. A Guide To The Elements, 2nd edition. New York, NY: Oxford University Press, Inc., 2002

Timmreck,   Roy S. Power Of The Periodic Table, Alameda, CA: Royal Palm Publishing, 1991

Young,   Robyn V. World of Chemistry. Famington Hills, MI: The Gale Group 2000

Journal Articles

Baum,   Rudy M. "Celebrating The Periodic Table." Chemical & Engineering News 81, 36 (2003); 27-190

Freemantle,   Michael. "Element 110 Named Darmstadtium." Chemical & Engineering News 81, 3 (2003): 11

Jacoby,   Mitch. "New Superheavy Elements Created." Chemical & Engineering News 82, 6 (2004): 7

Websites

Boorman,   Mollie and Husted, Robert. "Source: Los Alamos National Labs Chemistry Division," http//periodic.lanl.gov/default.htm (2003)

Manthey,   David. "Source: Orbial Central, Orbital Viewer-Ato,ic orbitals In All Their Glory," http://www.orbitals.com (2001)

Winter,   Mark J. "Source: WebElements,"http//www.webelements.com/ (2004)

Other

Jackson,   Mark D. "Chemistry (Quick Strudy Chart)." Boca Raton, FL: Barcharts, Inc. (2002)

Jackson,   Mark D. "Periodic Table of The Elements (Quick Study Chart)." Boca Raton, FL: Barcharts, Inc. (2002)

Periodic Table

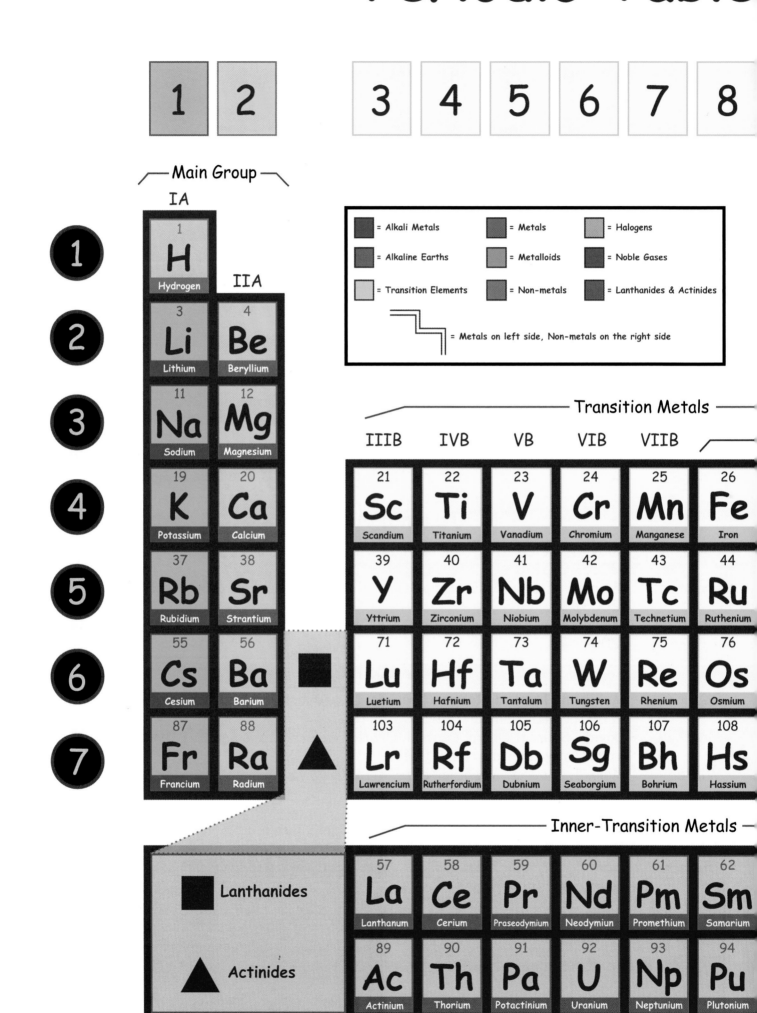

of the Elements

— Main Group —

VIIIA

		IB	IIB	IIIA	IVA	VA	VIA	VIIA	

| | | | | | | | | | 2 He Helium |

| | | | | 5 B Boron | 6 C Carbon | 7 N Nitrogen | 8 O Oxygen | 9 F Fluorine | 10 Ne Neon |

VIII

| | | | | 13 Al Aluminum | 14 Si Silicon | 15 P Phosphorus | 16 S Sulfur | 17 Cl Chlorine | 18 Ar Argon |

27 Co Cobalt	28 Ni Nickel	29 Cu Copper	30 Zn Zinc	31 Ga Gallium	32 Ge Germanium	33 As Arsenic	34 Se Selenium	35 Br Bromine	36 Kr Krypton
45 Rh Rhodium	46 Pd Palladium	47 Ag Silver	48 Cd Cadmium	49 In Indium	50 Sn Tin	51 Sb Antimony	52 Te Tellurium	53 I Iodine	54 Xe Xenon
77 Ir Iridium	78 Pt Platinum	79 Au Gold	80 Hg Mercury	81 Tl Thallium	82 Pb Lead	83 Bi Bismuth	84 Po Polonium	85 At Astatine	86 Rn Radon
109 Mt Meitnerium	110 Ds Darmstadtium	111 Rg Roentgenium	112 Uub Ununbium	113 Uut Ununtrium	114 Uuq Ununquadium	115 Uup Ununpentium	116 Uuh Ununhexium	117 Uus Ununseptium	118 Uuo Ununoctium

63 Eu Europium	64 Gd Gadolinium	65 Tb Terbium	66 Dy Dysprosium	67 Ho Holmium	68 Er Erbium	69 Tm Thulium	70 Yb Ytterbium
95 Am Americium	96 Cm Curium	97 Bk Berkelium	98 Cf Californium	99 Es Einsteinium	100 Fm Fermium	101 Md Mendelevium	102 No Nobelium

MACKStorm®
Productions, Inc.
www.MackStormProductions.com